Messages from the River

Jill Hance Bakke, EdD

Dedication

This book is dedicated to my daughters:

Beth Merie Slivkanch
Donna Lynn Mealy
Maura Ann Maneely
Kara Katrin Bakke

May your lives be enriched by nature and its beauty. May you always listen to your intuition, being aware of the messages given you by the universe. Thus, unfurl your sails and set your course with confidence.

To my old friend Joel with love - Jill

Contents

Prologue

I notice a thin ribbon of deep blue water lay against the Washington shore when I open the balcony door and step into the crisp September air. It has become a ritual to greet the river with my first cup of coffee in hand. As I sip my coffee, I stand watching the ribbon widen, pushing the blue water closer and closer to the Oregon shore until the entire width and visible length of the river reflects the great blue sky above.

This beautiful river, the Columbia, never fails to entrance me. Its diversity seems endless. Sailboats, kayaks, a paddle wheeler, Coast Guard ships, and cruise ships merge with the pilot boats, tugs, small fishing boats, and immense cargo and container ships that ply its waters. Sea lions, salmon, and occasional pods of whales mix with other sea life, and seagulls, crows, and cormorants rule the sky.

The landscape changes constantly. Whether the mournful sound of a big ship's foghorn, flotillas of Sunday fishermen stalking the salmon, loaded barges pulled by small tugs, or the wind-billowed mainsail of an individual sailboat, the view and its sounds capture my interest.

Earlier in the week, I had a phone call from a friend. During our conversation, he remarked, "You sound so relaxed. You need to keep hold of that place."

I have no intention of letting it go. When we discover our heart's place, we need to grab hold of it with both hands. Astoria and the Columbia River is my heart's place.

For generations, my family lived on the seacoast of the Atlantic Ocean. I grew up on New Jersey's Barnegat Bay and the sandy dunes of the Atlantic. After years of living in the rolling plains and mountains of the West, I hungered to return to the water. Moving to Astoria and the Columbia River was a homecoming.

Yet while the river's appearance of serenity brings me a sense of comfort, I have also come to know her as a swashbuckling giant. I am a Libra, so I see that balancing act in myself.

Let me introduce you.

The Columbia River

The Columbia River begins in British Columbia, Canada, and is approximately twelve hundred miles long. The native Chinook tribe called it *Wimahl*, or Big River. This description fits it well, for the Columbia is the largest river in the Pacific Northwest, the fourth largest river in North America, and the largest hydroelectric power-producing river in North America.

The Columbia Gorge acts as a funnel for the Columbia River. Because dangerous rapids at that location made any water transportation take to portage, the Cascade locks were completed in the Columbia Gorge in 1896. Later, in 1938, the original locks were submerged and replaced by Bonneville Lock and Dam. I recall standing at the Bonneville locks and finding three tiny clamshell fossils in the soil. I kept them for forty years, moving them from Montana to New Jersey and back west to Colorado. They are no bigger than a half-inch in length. Someday, I want to take passage on the paddle wheeler through the locks and up the Columbia River onto the Snake River, so there may be a book on the "rest of the story," as Paul Harvey used to say. For now, however, this book focuses on the river where I live.

Here in Astoria, the Columbia appears placid. But this is just its final pause before it gathers its power to roar into the Pacific. Ebb tides and the river's runoff create strong currents, and in stormy weather, waves have been measured between forty and seventy feet in height at the river's mouth.

The bar pilots, charged with the safety of ships passing through the dangerous entrance, board and exit the commercial ships near the Astoria-Megler Bridge and in the Pacific Ocean. Whether exiting or entering, the trip through the bar is dangerous; from the beginning of its navigation, the Columbia bar has been considered a major part of what is commonly known as the Graveyard of the Pacific.

The actual graveyard area also includes the rocky shoreline of the west coast of Vancouver Island, the shores of the Olympic Peninsula, and the Strait of Juan de Fuca (www.geocaching.com/geocache/ GC1JMEY graveyard-of-the-pacific).

While on the river, pilots normally board by ladder from a pilot boat. Both boats are moving, and the climb can be as much as sixty feet. The pilots on the ocean side use a helicopter or the pilot boats, *Astoria* and *Columbia*, for boarding and exiting, and their state-of-the-art equipment allows the bar pilots to take and return control of vessels farther from the entrance to the dangerous Columbia River.

Pier 39
Based on photo by Jiill Hance Bakke

The windows of my condo overlook Pier 39 and Astoria's East Basin with a view that extends downstream to the Astoria-Megler Bridge and upstream to Tongue's Point. This stretch includes moored ships waiting to either proceed up river or exit to the ocean. Here the pilots exchange duties, moving the command of a commercial ship from bar pilot to river pilot (or the other way around). Most days, I see five or six anchored cargo and container ships on the river along with other commercial vessels, which include a few tugs with their barges, and a mixture of other boats; inside the seawall, fishing boats and small craft share the docks.

The view provides an enjoyable mix of town and river. The Astoria trolley line ends at the foot of Pier 39. This pier contains the oldest and largest waterfront building in Astoria, 84,800 square feet of covered space. Originally built in 1870 as a Bumble Bee packing plant, it was one of many similar fish-packing plants that blossomed along the river in Astoria.

The Hanthorn Cannery Foundation, which is dedicated to the preservation of the canning industry, has restored the building, and it now houses the Fisherman's Suites (inviting rentals with incredible views), Coffee Girl with its delicious food and coffee, Rouge Ales Public House, offices, and museums. Astoria Scuba, renting diving equipment, kayaks, and paddleboards, is also located there. Pier 39 speaks of the old and the new, the unchanging and the changing, as does the trolley.

The Astoria Trolley began its first trip on June 8, 1999, using tracks purchased from Burlington Northern, when the freight rail line from Portland to Astoria was abandoned in 1996. The trolley runs along the river with its last stop at the foot of Pier 39. The trip costs little and offers other views of the beautiful and busy Columbia River, including the historic Uppertown Net Loft.

Built in 1900 by the Union Fishermen's Cooperative Packing Company, the Uppertown Net Loft is a reminder of the Columbia River's salmon, fishing, and canning industry that fueled the growth of Astoria in the late 1800s and early 1900s. It was built as a net drying and mending shed, hence the name Net Loft. Natural fiber nets, which often were made in the fishermen's homes during the winters, needed to be dried between uses. Fishermen could navigate their boats right up under the building, where a hoist would lift the nets to dry. The building can be seen in the water at Thirty-First Street in Astoria. Storms have heavily damaged the structure, but its charm and beauty remain.

Uppertown Net Loft
Based on photo by Jill Hance Bakke

While the 1913 trolley car, nicknamed "Old 300," is well worth the ride and its views and history fascinating, it is the river that continually draws me. The geography of the river, its venture into fishing and logging, the story of Astoria itself, Pier 39, and the trolley are not the purpose of these pages. My purpose is to share what the river reminds me of: what it shows me, teaches me, and gives to me. It reminds me of who I am and what I should be. It may say something else to someone else, but I suspect many readers will relate to the messages I have received from the river.

Weather, fog, sunsets, the moon and tides, and the activity on the river bring me into meetings with myself. Each topic stands alone and can be used as the focus of a meditation or as a thread to explore in your own journal, but this is not a "how-to" book; there are no formal instructions.

Everyone has a muse, something that acts as a source of inspiration, something that makes them reflect, meditate, or consider in silent wonder. The Columbia River is my muse.

What speaks to you? Wind and rain? The moon and stars? The flowers brightly blooming in a garden, or is it the smile of a child, the soaring notes of music, or the beauty of architecture that draws you near self?

Let your muse guide you into expression. Write a poem. Draw pictures. Compose some music. Take photographs. Sculpt in clay. Make a collage. Create something unique to represent the offerings from your muse.

My muse has led me to this book. Most of my messages are short, but not all. Read them as a book or read one a day.

I hope you will discover your own dialog developing with the material in this book and find your own ideas surfacing to be explored. Follow whatever threads those thoughts offer.

I start with a place marker. The first message begins as I return to Oregon after closing on the condo by mail. It is September, and it is my birthday. The year is 2014. My daughter has picked me up at the Portland airport, and I am spending the night with her. I think of the first message as setting the stage.

Part I
Messages from the River

Astoria overlooking the Columbia River
Based on photo by Kara Bakke

Chapter 1

In the Beginning

Excited about moving into my new condo on the Columbia River, my daughter and I are engrossed in our conversation. We've talk so much coming in from the airport that we miss our exit. The GPS comes out of hiding, and Mrs. GPS starts her instructions: exit here, turn left, and we wind our way home, the road unfurling in a black-and-white ribbon before us. When the car pulls into the driveway of my daughter's home, we are still talking.

Sleep comes easily and sweetly this night as I snuggle under the covers. I awake in the morning with a dog lying at my feet, a cat in my window, and the smell of coffee brewing. Genuinely content, I considered the events of the night before and decide that being in touch with spirit is much like using the GPS. When we feel confused or discouraged, spirit is always there to show us our way.

I can't help but wonder why I have such confidence in Mrs. GPS's directions but so often have difficulty with my own intuition. It is especially hard when I am certain I know exactly what I want. I recently learned, however, what I want is not always what is best for me. I don't always see a situation clearly.

Several months earlier, when I was unable to buy a house in Cannon Beach that I wanted, I was devastated. The owners had accepted a lower offer ahead of mine, with the condition that the prospective buyers could opt out when they physically viewed the property if they didn't like it. The original offer went through despite the fact I tried everything to change the situation. I bought pillows for the house and claimed it as mine. I offered more money. I prayed. I cried. I said affirmations. I was so involved that I couldn't see another

1

option in housing for me; I left no space for intuition to enter. I was literally batting my head against the proverbial wall. I thought I'd never find another dwelling I liked as well. And I was certain I wanted to live in Cannon Beach.

However, a few months later, another house came on the market in Astoria. I knew nothing about Astoria, but the house tempted me. On examination, there were major construction problems that made the house unsuitable. But Astoria wasn't. I loved Astoria. Only one remaining problem: a dwelling I liked.

When I saw this place I now call home, I realized I didn't want a second house with all its upkeep and big gardens to care for. A house with gardens was no longer right for me. I had always said I *never* wanted a condo, but I wanted this one with its big windows that opened to the Columbia River and filled the north-facing unit with light. High ceilings and a loft bedroom created a vision of great space without a lot of maintenance.

Instead of weeding and pruning a garden, I chose a deck filled with flowers, and comfortable chairs and table. The Columbia River runs past my balcony. It bustles with industry. Not only is it peaceful, but the town has charm, and the sunsets arrive with incredible beauty.

I understand, but sometimes forget, that if I listen and trust, then I can relax. And if I can relax, I can listen and trust. I am always guided.

Time to get up. The dog already has. Miss Kitty will nap here all day. I could rummage through my life and add to my list of examples of guidance from spirit if I so choose, but I smell coffee.

Chapter 2

Moored vessels outside sheltered harbor
Based on photo by Jill Hance Bakke

Mooring

I open the door and wander outside, with my first cup of coffee in hand. The mighty Columbia River intrigues me. I welcome it each morning and bid it good night before heading to bed.

Today, the river's surface is quiet, as if waiting. The moored ships lie still. The scene appears much the same as yesterday, yet different. Four big ships are moored in front my home. The cruise ship is gone. The sea lions are quieter. One huge container ship begins to move down the Columbia towards the ocean, silently, with little wake and slow speed. A tiny pilot boat is tucked by its side to transfer the bar pilot aboard. I wonder what the moored ships wait for. One has been my silent companion for over a week, just floating on the river, waiting. I am amused by the name emblazoned on its side, *De Amigo*. By now, it does feel like my friend, and I find myself curious as to what the crew does during these long periods of waiting.

My life has periods like this: periods of waiting, periods when nothing seems to be moving. When I lived in Montana, I thought of such times as mesas, those treeless flat-top land formations that existed in the Montana plains and rolling hills. Life was "same old, same old." Here, I think of them as moorings. They don't feel like the flat tops I called mesas. Those were lifeless times. These feel more like a tree that is putting down roots and anchoring itself in rich soil. Mesas made me antsy. Moorings give me peace. In one, I wanted to be actively doing, but here I simply want to be.

Why was it so hard for me to just be? Why couldn't I live in the peace of the moment in Montana? There, I felt a need to create a world of distractions. It was easy to be busy and pretend I was in control. I would charge into each new thing with passion, yet often ended up in exhaustion. All that activity seeking something but gaining nothing. The ships are not seeking; they are simply waiting. The tides come and go and do not budge them. Other ships pass and do not disturb them. When the call comes, the ships lift anchor and move out to sea or up the river.

Perhaps being moored is an inside job. Ships drop anchor like the trees put down roots. Then they rest quietly. I put down my anchor when I stop and listen and watch the world around me, when I meditate or pray, and yes, when I ponder the world, as I am now doing. These types of things anchor me to my spirit and fill me with the nourishment I need when I am called to move and be in the world. How did I reach this point of anchoring myself to my spirit? How can others reach their place of peace and contentment? Is it something I did or did it just happen?

I find myself considering if being in one's natural element has something to do with it. Watery elements have always drawn me. I feel at home around them. I grew up on Barnegat Bay and the Atlantic Ocean. My ancestors on both sides as far back as before the Revolutionary War lived on this same bay and ocean. Could my DNA be calling me to water?

I once read a story in Clarissa Pinkola Estés' *Women Who Run with Wolves*. The tale is of a seal that comes onto land and sheds her skin. She is referred to as a "selkie." A lonely man who sees her beauty wants her for his wife. He knows if he can hide her skin, she must stay with him. So, one night, he steals her sealskin and buries it under an overturned boat. She marries the man, and they have a child. But eventually, she finds her sealskin and returns to the sea. I immediately related to her. She, like me, always longed for her true nature. I sometimes call myself a " selkie." Montana, as beautiful as it is, never felt like home. Some part of me was being traded away in that location.

But I believe this environmental link represents only one element. Perhaps this missing environmental link had to be coupled with learning to love myself enough to say no to things that no longer serve me. Was that the key to my peace?

I don't want to romanticize that part of the journey. Some of it was damn hard when I had to do it. A house I loved. A man I loved. Work that had been fulfilling but no longer was. There came a time when they no longer served me and had to be released. Perhaps these acts of releasing are part of the difference between a mesa and a mooring.

Here on the Columbia, watching the flow of the water and the moored boats, I feel a spiritual connection to my environment of choice and a willingness to release outworn things. It is this combination that creates my feeling of mooring, a feeling of coming home.

Everyone's journey is different. Everyone must find his own way. My understandings for where I am on my journey will not fit everyone. That is okay. They fit me.

Chapter 3

Diversity

I have been watching the boats on the Columbia for three weeks now. The activity fascinates me. The commercial river traffic comes in all shapes and sizes. At night, when moored, they light up like Christmas trees. When they travel, they dim the lights and move swiftly through the water, steered through the sandbars by the bar and river pilots.

The river is alive with its traffic. A cruise ship, a National Geographic vessel, and a Coast Guard ship dock side by side, like three peas in a pod. The fishing boats add color, with blue or white hulls predominating. Trawlers with their big nets wound on spools at the back of their boats lie peacefully alongside boats without that adornment. Small motorboats, rowboats, kayaks, and even paddleboards find their way close to the shipping lanes. Frequently, I see a lone sailboat with its pristine white sails maneuvering in the wind through the moored container and cargo ships. One night, close to midnight, I watched the large Mississippi-type paddleboat leave its mooring and head up to Portland. Today, I saw an old gray naval ship making its way out towards the ocean. And frequently, there are barges pushed or pulled along by mighty tugboats.

How many different sizes and shapes exist in harmony on the river? Here, space and acceptance exist for every possible type of floating object. Wildlife is included in their space. The sea lions live a few blocks away. There are far too many of them to count. Sometimes a group of them come and visit me, living on the rocks in front of my window while conducting a vocal party that runs 24/7. Seabirds, gulls, herons, double-breasted cormorants, ducks, and other birds ply the water. Scuba divers in their dark wetsuits also paddle around in the waters near the pier.

Can I allow such diversity into my life? Diversity doesn't mean I cannot have my preferences. But if I can acknowledge that differences make life interesting, and if I am receptive to them, wouldn't I enjoy life more?

Chapter 4

Path along Alderbrook Cove
Based on photo by Jill Hance Bakke

Hidden Gifts

There exists along the river coves where hidden gifts of nature's beauty flourish. One such cove lies just east of my condo. No boats go here in its shallow waters (unless, for some reason, someone puts a small canoe into the water). This cove looks limited and very tiny and appears insignificant in comparison to the river's commanding strength.

Two sides of the cove are heavily sheltered with towering trees and undergrowth; then it opens to a fringe of vegetation before the greenery thickens and it begins to curve back towards the main river bed. The Riverwalk continues across the mouth of this tiny cove, over a short wooden bridge that still bears old train rails. The view from the bridge is pleasant but not unusual. The remnants of either an old dock or submerged trees peek their wooden heads up through the water where the natural growth is thickest. A few houses stand on a slight rise before the cove narrows to rejoin the larger river.

A path splits off from the Riverwalk just before the bridge crosses the cove. It looks untraveled, and from the Riverwalk, one cannot see far down this path. Tall trees arch branches over the walkway. It looks lonely and dangerous. Where does it lead? It is a mystery. Is it safe for a woman to venture along it alone? Such thoughts come naturally to mind.

One day, I dare to investigate it, only to discover hidden treasures abound along the path. That first time, the bushes are covered with golden blossoms that both soar skyward and hang in graceful arches. Where least expected, wild, yellow iris rise from damp, moist soil in hidden pockets. I see bamboo grass just beginning its stretch towards the sun; moss clinging to trees; and green, wild ivy trailing here and there. Fragrant green growth is everywhere.

I begin to take the path frequently and watch the beauty change. The vivid yellow of the iris and tall brilliant bushes give way to clusters of tiny white flowers that bloom in swaths along the sides of the path. Patches of wild violets show their faces in unexpected places. Big, white star-like flowers that blossom on sprawling bushes and other plants that remain nameless to me later follow.

Then, as summer turns into fall and the days grow cooler, blackberry bushes ripe with fruit make their appearance. I feel blessed to have found this beautiful place, and Frost's poem "The Road Not Taken" comes to mind. How often we refuse to step into the unknown. How much I would have missed if I hadn't moved beyond my fears and explored this path.

But this was not the main message the river gave to me about this experience. As I focused on the gifts of beauty, I realized that I too have personality aspects and soul qualities I do not show to everyone. Sometimes, others must have patience with me before I show my gifts. I think I keep things hidden because of fear: fear they are not good enough to share, fear they are unusual and will not be accepted.

Perhaps that one hidden gift many of us subconsciously or consciously seek is our connection to spirit or soul or something larger and bigger than the dogma of religion, something more personal and healing. Yet this was the one gift I held closest to my heart for many years. The river made me acknowledge it was time to let it rise to the surface, time for me to allow my gifts to be seen, whether they are a talent or a quality like faith and patience.

Our gifts are as varied as the gifts of the river, but unlike the river, which freely expresses them, ours await our invitation. The river has no fears of exposing its gifts. It cares not that some people call the gifts of gold and white flowers weeds. The river doesn't judge the beauty of the path with its sweeping carpet of flowers as less important than the river's work of carrying the big ships. The river considers all gifts equal, none more important or needed than another. In the same way, each of our gifts is important and needs to be shared.

I recognized that my note to a sick friend is as important a gift as writing this book or volunteering in a soup kitchen. As I deliver from my nature, the connection to my inner guide and to something that is bigger than me grows. More and more gifts come forth until I, like this river, overflow with resources and beauty. This is the gift of the creator to us, and it is available to each of us.

I too need to nurture my gifts as the river nurtures the land. I can nurture them initially by acknowledging them with gratitude and allowing them to surface instead of staying hidden. Some may require my attention, weeding out elements that attempt to strangle them. I may have to explore other roads, even if I am uncertain as to where they will lead. I am up to this task.

Today, I bless the river for its message and turn within to ask myself, what hidden gifts am I growing? What new interests and passions are calling to me? How can I help them grow? I will no longer hide.

Chapter 5

Fog

The river continues to teach me. The evening is foggy. I can barely see the ships moored outside my window. They are ghost ships. The world appears in silent, muted colors. Even the sea lions are subdued. Nothing stands out in sharp relief. Gray water is welded to gray sky. Gray water. Gray sky. Gray fog. Here and there, pinpoints of light shine from the moored ships.

The river has created another replica of life that sometimes appears in our journeys. Yet there is always that tiny bit of light that cannot be squelched. Like the ones on the ships and the light in my window tonight, they provide enough light to find our way. I go to bed, snug under the covers, and sleep without dreaming.

Awakening shows a thicker fog lying denser over the river than it did last night. Today, I can see only the buildings on the pier directly in front of my building. Yet as I look inland, the fog has lightened, and visibility is much better. It doesn't seem to affect the cars traveling by or people walking down the street. Only the water and its surroundings are cocooned in the soft, thick, gray blanket of fog.

Have you ever been in a situation where one area of life feels hazy, uncertain? I have. Which way shall I go? Where will the road lead me? Should I wait it out until I can see the steps I should take? How long will that take? Should I turn and go the land route so many others are following?

Unknown spaces in life can be frightening. I wonder why? In the fog that lies before me, I know if I go just this far, just over the pier to the coffee shop, I may see a bit farther into the thick fog. The lights that still glow in the fog will become clearer as I venture into it. In the fog outside my windows, I know what is there, although I cannot see it. I anticipate the fog will lift by noon; the sun will burn it away. But, in life, there are no such guarantees, and with the fogs in our personal spaces, we often don't know what is there or when it will dissipate.

In everyday life, I have fogs within my personal spaces. These are times when I need to make a decision and know not what to do. Of course, I could do nothing. That is a decision. I could also stay and watch until it clears, which may cause me to be late in acting. Or, I could take the shrouded path, one that is still somewhat unknown.

Even when I am thrown into making a decision that appears to have no good choice, my job is to hold the thought that my way will be made clear one step at a time, as I quiet my mind, listen to my intuition, and quietly edge into the fog.

There are patches of blue sky now. I can see farther, almost to the opposite shore. And I realize I have gained the firm belief that if I take the fogs of my life step by step, slowly feeling out the terrain, life will eventually clear all the fog of my indecision, like the sun burns away the thick gray fog.

I must remind myself daily: "*Take that one little step you can see, Jill. The next step will become clear.*"

Chapter 6

Whitecaps

Although usually placid in front of my condo, the Columbia River is rough today. Small whitecaps ride the tops of the gray waves. The fishing boats bob at their docks. Only the large freighters remain unmoving on the river. Fog is rolling in, and the rain has come in inconsistent showers throughout the day. The condo feels the chill of the damp and dreary day, and I turn to the fireplace for warmth.

When things are in turmoil, do I act like the river's white-capped waves, or can I remain unmoving? There are so many things in our world that disturb us: new diseases like Ebola, financial fluctuations, terrorist attacks, and shootings in schools. Do I allow these upsetting events to make my energy as rippling waves with foaming peaks? When my energy is distraught, scattered, or unfocused, I cannot help others. I become disassociated from my inner self, that spirit piece we all possess. Solutions and directions cannot be heard.

When I remain calm under stress, it helps calm those around me. I need to remember I have a choice as to my reaction. I can be the silent, unmoving freighter or the churning, frothing water. This image from the river speaks to me. It tells me to stay calm and seek connection to my source. Then, like the ships, I will be deeply and safely moored and able to help moor those around me.

Chapter 7

After the storm
Base on photo by Kara Bakke

This Too Shall Pass

It had been raining slow and heavy most of the day, making pit holes in the river's surface, when just before dusk, the water turned wild. Out of nowhere, a wind whipped up, sending me scurrying to my deck to grab the geranium, which was about to crash on the concrete floor. Plant and planter rescued, door latched, I curled up on the sofa to watch the mounting storm.

I watched a lone bird struggle past my windows, seeking safety as the howling winds whipped the river into waves. And although the roof of my condo echoed the sounds of wind and rain through my loft, the storm and the river were playing greater havoc with the freighters. One massive ship changed her mooring twice to ease the ship's rolling, as the winds continued to pick up.

Finally, as dusk turned into night, the winds quieted some, allowing the river to find some ease from the agitation the winds created. However, the storm continued off and on throughout the night, with silence and calm interspersed with the pounding rain and sudden demanding winds. I could no longer see the water's reaction in the darkness, so I gave in to the storm's angry, wet tantrum and went to bed.

Sometime during the dark hours, the wind died, and the storm lightened. By sunrise, there was a light fog, which quickly cleared, leaving the day drenched in sunshine. The water lay quiet. It looked as if the angry, rolling river had never been. I stood on my balcony, soaking in the peace and calm while the river murmured in my head, "Sure, it was rough, but it always passes."

And it always passes for humans, if we allow it.

Chapter 8

Wind and rain
Based on photo by Kara Bakke

Judgment and Surrender

Storm clouds lie on the horizon. The water and sky will soon meet in shades of gray today. When the rain pelts down on the roof of my condo and makes little pit marks where it hits the water below, I decide to forego the trip into town that I had planned. The river is otherwise quiet, and I am staying inside, peacefully curled up in a chair by the cozy fire. It is as if both my river and I have surrendered to the weather.

Neither judgment nor surrender have been easy tasks for me to accomplish. But during these past few years, I have improved. I think it is because I looked at situations where I fought what was because I wanted something different. All I got from those efforts was a headache. From a distance, things that immediately seemed bad, difficult, or unnecessary have proven the exact opposite. They carried huge gifts I would otherwise never have been given if I had not learned to stop labeling events and fighting what is.

Now when faced with events I cannot control, I simply let them play out. It doesn't mean I don't do what I can. If I am sick, I will go to doctors and try their remedies if they feel right to me. But I no longer focus on the negative aspects of the events. I give up the "poor me" syndrome and the "I want" attitude and make myself as comfortable as I can in the circumstances I am facing.

Doing this helps me the most; I am no longer stuck in the middle or feeling as though I was slogging through mud. No more attitude of "I don't like this. Come hell or high water, I am going to change it." Instead, I surrender to those things out of my control—things like the weather, a health issue, or a project I don't want to handle that has been thrust in my lap.

It takes courage and strength to find the hidden gifts in some experiences, but it is far easier if I don't label my experiences. I have always liked an old Taoist teaching story that I will share here. It didn't mean an awful lot to me until I was willing to look at what I had labeled as "bad" things in my life and weighed the end results of those bad happenings. Each carried a gift, a gift I was glad to receive.

Just reading this and saying, "Oh that is a nice ending," doesn't mean mastery of the art of nonjudgmental surrender. Some of the things that happen—a divorce, loss of a job, or severe health issues—can be extremely painful when they occur. But I assure you if you are willing to look, not judge them, and to surrender and wait, there will be a gift given you from the trial and tribulation.

A Taoist Teaching Story

The old farmer had worked his crops for many years. Then one day, his horse ran away. Upon hearing the news, his neighbors came to visit. "Such bad luck," they said sympathetically.

"Maybe," the farmer replied.

The next morning, the horse returned, bringing with it three wild horses.

"How wonderful," the neighbors exclaimed.

"Maybe," replied the old man.

The following day, his son tried to ride one of the untamed horses, was thrown, and broke his leg.

The neighbors again came to offer their sympathy for his misfortune.

"Maybe," answered the farmer.

The day after, military officials came to the village to draft young men into the army. Seeing that the son's leg was broken, they passed him by. The neighbors congratulated the farmer on how good things had turned out.

"Maybe," said the farmer.

The story tells us of a man who did not judge what was happening to him but simply accepted it and waited to see how it turned out.

We use our minds to make our way through the world, and we seem to be made up of judgments. Being rich is better than not being rich. This is a lousy job. I need to have [you fill in the blank] if I am happy. I don't like my neighbor because he is always [you fill in the blank]. How awful that Jane's engagement was broken.

One of our common judgments is I can't do [whatever]. So, we never attempt to develop or accomplish that task, even when we wanted to and could have learned how to accomplish it. We name it *I can't*, and so it is.

The Taoists are not the only group with an injunction about judging. The Bible gives its direction in Matthew 7:1–2 (NIV):

"Do not judge, or you too will be judged. For in the same way you judge others, you will be judged, and with the measure you use, it will be measured to you."

What I decide something is—and thus give it a name—it literally becomes that for me. If I call an action evil, I have difficulty looking beyond the label to understand its causation and let compassion grow. If I label something bad, I will shun it and not seek its message. I may even go into the victim role, which never serves a good purpose. If I call an illness incurable, it usually will be. And if I look around, I will discover that what I call good, someone else will say is bad, and what I call unnecessary, someone else will need.

We all work from old labels that are based on our experience and early patterning from our parents and the culture in which we live.

What is, is. I must learn not to label. I must stay in the "maybe" spot. 1 Corinthians 13:12 tells of seeing through a glass darkly. How can I judge accurately when I don't see clearly? I'm content in here on a rainy day, although I had wanted to go downtown. If I called my change of plans bad, I would not have found contentment. It is as simple as that.

Chapter 9

The Underbelly

This morning, the river is showing me its underbelly. The full moon last night has drawn the tides far down, and muddy spots in the great Columbia River look up at my windows. The river itself seems to take no notice of the way it looks. It is indifferent to its appearance. The ships lay moored as always. The fishing boats remain tied to their docks, the water placid around the pilings of the pier.

I don't find this underbelly very attractive, but the seabirds seem to like this change of tides. They wade around in the muddy shallow with great intensity, finding delicacies that the river seldom serves them for breakfast. No one else seems to notice the underbelly. The joggers on the path below my window don't turn their heads to stare. They never even look.

I think about the deep scar on my right forearm. For over forty years, I have kept that scar under cover. Only my closest friends and family ever see it. Even in the heat of summer, I wear a light shirt over it most of the time. To me, it looks ugly, like the underbelly of the river. I wonder what else I am keeping under cover so what I deem ugly or embarrassing to me might not be visible to others.

Perhaps what I see as ugly is not ugly at all. Perhaps what embarrasses me does not affect others at all. Like the underbelly of the river that suddenly appeared, just maybe, there is good living in what has been hidden. Perhaps I should do some personal excavating today. What am I hiding that should come into the light? What needs my loving acceptance?

Chapter 10

**Bar pilot boats, the *Astoria* and the
Columbia, docked in Hammond, OR**
Based on photo by Jill Hance Bakke

The Bar Pilots

The mighty Columbia isn't a gentle rolling river, settling into an unchanging riverbed. The river's size and power allow her to shift the sand beneath her, and her power grows as she approaches the outlet to the Pacific Ocean. There, at the Columbia Bar, she becomes a rolling, howling, swashbuckling force of nature that demands honor and respect from all who seek to pass through. In a five-minute span, her disposition can change from calm to life-threatening, as her currents change due to wind and ocean swells.

The Columbia Bar has rightfully earned the name Graveyard of the Pacific. Her waters can morph into giant standing waves, forty-five feet and higher. Her challenging currents can push their prey into the sandbars, leaving them stranded for the waves to eat away their ribs and stays.

Part of the year I live alongside this magnificent river in Astoria. She is my muse; I think of her simply as River. But today, my mind moves to her pilots, those individuals who are charged with helping the ships move in and out of her mouth.

The river is deceptively quiet where I live. After guiding a vessel the hazardous miles through the bar, the bar pilots turn the massive ships over to Columbia River pilots, who guide the vessels through narrow channels to Portland and other stops. Still, even in these quieter waters, as pilots embark or disembark, they must climb the side of the moving cargo ship on a rope ladder from—or to—a small pilot boat running alongside it. Some ships are so large that the rope dangling between the moving boats requires a sixty-foot climb. This alone is a courageous feat to me. But the true story of courage comes at the mouth of the Columbia.

Bar pilots must be knowledgeable as well as courageous to pilot the ships between the ocean entrance buoy and the inland side of the Astoria-Megler Bridge. These men and women (Capt. Deborah Dempsey was a pilot from 1994 to her retirement in 2016) need to be quick-witted and able to make immediate judgments under pressure. Requirements to become a bar pilot on the Columbia are one of the highest in the United States. These requirements include holding an unlimited Master Mariner's license and serving two years as master of an oceangoing vessel of at least 5,000 gross tons. According to the Bar Pilots Association, this means that they have been at sea between 15 and 25 years.

Pilots must understand both the physical territory of the bar in detail and the temperament of the river to guide vessels as wide as a hundred feet and as long as three football fields through the six-hundred-foot-wide channel. Thus, in addition to being able to draw a map of the entrance from memory, a bar pilot trainee must complete 100 crossing in the presence of a licensed pilot to prove knowledge and ability.

Before entering the mouth of the Columbia, the bar pilots usually board by a helicopter, which bears the name Skyhawk. This method leaves them dangling in a harness above the deck until they can safely jump onto the ship. When the weather is bad, and the helicopter cannot fly, two sturdy seventy-two-foot pilot boats, the *Columbia* and *Astoria*, which are moored at Hammond, put the pilots onboard. The pilots board by rope ladder, often with the pilot boat holding course through waves that sweep over its deck.

Nowhere can ships expect taller waves than at the entrance to the mouth of the Columbia. The channel is dredged, but the sand spits on the sides remain littered with old wrecks. In addition, the dogleg turn in the treacherous channel adds its own menace.

What draws people to this work of piloting across the bar? What creates their courage? What displaces their fears of injury and death? Why am I drawn to them? They have no fear of the risks. They have prepared themselves to handle whatever may come, and they love their work.

Most people who reap success are willing to take risks. Am I drawn to the bar pilots because there are areas in my life where I need to be a risk-taker? I find myself wondering what I fear; where do I lack the courage to move ahead in areas that I love? What holds me back? How can I move to take the risks involved? I need to think on this.

For photos and videos of bar pilots at work, go to http://www.columbiariverbarpilots.com/# and http://www.columbiariverpilots.com

Chapter 11

Sea Lions on Rocks
Based on photo by Jill Hance Bakke

Conformity

Sea lions have become a calling card for Astoria. Tourists delight in walking down to the docks, where the sea lions rest. There are so many of them, tightly packed one against the other, that it is impossible to accurately count them. They are not individualist, they conform, rest in colonies when on land and gather in rafts when traveling in the water. One voice might be louder than the another's, yet the barking sounds are similar.

But the Columbia River is a nonconformist. It is strong, determined, and constantly changing. Why am I not more like the river? Why do so many of us conform? What do we fear that makes us build little boxes in which we live? To use an old phrase, we are a nation of sheep. Why are we afraid to be different?

The bar pilots are certainly different. They face danger and the unexpected with calm. I doubt few if any fears assail them. They can't fear failure, injury, or death and do the work they do. And they've chosen work that is very different from the norm. Obviously, there is a wild child in them who loves the challenge, knows what it can accomplish, and is ready and willing to be different.

Somewhere, hidden in my overlay of social graces and cultural programming, I too have a wild child. We all do. Our wild children don't usually choose the physically dangerous, but all wild children feast on the unexpected: the move that is nonsensical to others. Those of us who are lucky find the ability to use the wild child in our work as well as our play.

The wild child shows up in Freud's psychology theories, in Frank Lloyd Wright's architecture, and the Campbell soup paintings that brought Andy Warhol's name before the public. It appears as well in the brilliance of Leonardo da Vinci, who died in 1519, but conceptualized double hulled boats, armored vehicles, flying machines, and other inventions that were not built until centuries after his death. The wild child is present when we are willing to be different, willing to march to our own drummer and let our true self be known.

Although our wild child may not want action as challenging and dangerous as that of a bar pilot, they may appear as unusual to those around us. A wild child may show up in the way we look, the work we do, or how we live.

The wild child of nonconformity seems to be in the blood of every individual who has changed the world in some way. Edison, Einstein, and the Wright brothers were anything but conformists. Picasso and Walt Whitman lived unconventional lives, and in their artistic creations they gave us new views of the society in which we lived, while changing the genres in which they created: art and poetry. Bill Gates, a National Merit Scholar, enrolled in Harvard only to drop out and change the computer industry.

Nonconformists have many different faces, but many of them hold one characteristic in common: the need for introspection. Some chose to leave society for a while, like Eckhart Tolle, who for about two years sat on park benches in Russell Square, Central London, watching the world go by. He was considered odd and irresponsible, but rose to be one of the world's leading spiritual teachers and to write a series of books, including *The Power of Now: A Guide to Spiritual Enlightenment* and *A New Earth: Awakening to Your Life's Purpose*.

Joseph Campbell deliberately left society to spend a year reading the classics. He is best known for his work in applying mythology to our daily lives and for coining the two well-known phrases: "follow your bliss" and "the hero's journey."

Others were forcibly removed from society; Sadat, Mandela, and Gandhi were imprisoned before they emerged as leaders of their countries. Galileo, who would not recant his belief, was imprisoned by the Church for saying the sun, not the earth, was the center of the universe.

Those who change the world have found their calling and with it the strength to act upon its demands of being different. Out of each sabbatical, regardless of how it occurred, came wisdom shared with the world. Not all totally withdrew, but each had to look within. Looking within has many forms. Some people do it in meditation, others in dreaming. We can go within in the solitude of nature. Each of us will have his or her own preferable way, and it may well be one I have not mentioned here.

Men are not the only world changers. Women also have taken the road of life-changing nonconformity. It took from 1848 to 1920 before all the states ratified the constitutional amendment giving women the right to vote. This period of struggle, led by Elizabeth Cady Stanton and Susan B. Anthony, saw years of mockery, hardship, and even imprisonment for the women who banded together to get the amendment passed.

Many, like Stanton, Anthony, and the women who worked with them, paid a steep price for their nonconformity, but many others paid the full price. Joan of Arc was burned at the stake. Abraham Lincoln and Egypt's Anwar el-Sadat were assassinated. Jesus was crucified. Fortunately, few of us are asked to pay such heavy prices as imprisonment or death.

However, there is a price we pay if we squelch the wild child who seeks something different from what we consider to be the norm. Few of us are asked to change the world. We are simply asked to become authentic, to be as we were created to be.

I have seen what occurs when we don't. A good friend of mine wanted to be a marine architect. His family talked him into becoming involved in the family business like the other men in the family. But it didn't satisfy him to just be a weekend boater, and he turned out broke, addicted, divorced, and living an unhappy life. It seems we need to follow our heart when the wild child calls, especially when the longings are strong.

Knowing this, I must ask myself: "Why do I cling so hard to the shore of conformity, of being part of the crowd? Why am I so hesitant to move beyond my fears? "I never wanted to be different. I wonder why so few escape that reaction. Such a fear is probably more detrimental than any other because if I conform, I cannot be my authentic self.

I am making a vow: I will follow my own longings, my own direction, and not fit into the boxes others create for me. What an adventure I will have, as I follow my heart's desires.

Chapter 12

Polestar

A large cargo vessel lays moored outside my condo. She has been christened *Polestar*, her name emblazoned in bold letters across her side. I love the word. In a way, it fits this sturdy ship that has held my interest these past two days.

Yet the word "polestar" means more than a casual center of attraction; it refers to a guiding principle. It is the central core of what we seek at any given time. It is our compass, our guide; it determines our direction. I find myself turning inward as I look at the letters on the ship: *Polestar*. What is my polestar or guiding light now in my life's journey? We all require a polestar if we are to experience true happiness.

At one time, my focus centered on raising my daughters. At another, it centered on my education. These areas were polestars. I knew each step to take and what was most important. Knowing what is important is to know our polestar. Following that direction gives us authenticity. Authenticity is my goal.

I know what my polestar is now, but I seek to delve deeper into the core of this thing that draws me so deeply into knowing myself, who I am, what I am. I want to learn what skills I still need to polish to be truly effective for self and others. I want to know what step is the best for me to take now.

The universe gives directions when asked. I decide to spend some time working with this in meditation and my journal today.

Chapter 13

Wildflowers growing at river's edge
Based on photo by Jill Hance Bakke

Magic

Last night, as I usually do, I walked out on my deck to say good night to the river. I stood silently enraptured by her beauty. The sky was dark, but the river sparkled with the lights from the container ships moored in her waters. And in front of me, a street light on the pier acted like the moon and laid a shimmering path on her surface, while the waves lapped her banks with the ocean's song.

I walk along her banks today, taking pictures and admiring the wild and not-so-wild flowers. I glance at the big red house that sits at river's feet and whose deck leans over her waters. How wonderful, I think, to be that close to the river.

I spy a four-inch-long slug slowly making its way across the edge of the path into the grass's protection and stop to watch the double-crested cormorants and herons on the water. I know the river's message today. It is reminding me of the multitude of beauty in the natural world and the sacredness of all nature.

Magic

Beautiful River wearing
a ribbon of gold,
singing mermaid songs
as the wind kisses your skin.

While on your breast,
the big ships rest and
down on Pier 36,
sea lions party all night long.

Part II
Messages from the Universe

Heron
Based on photo by Kevin Danishefsky

Chapter 14

The Queen of Hearts

Each of us is on a journey, and sometimes, we desperately want direction. We can deliberately look for messages from a source that attracts us, one that speaks to our hearts. I have done this with the Columbia River. But the universe delivers her messages to us in many ways. She is determined to get those message across. Even when we do not listen, she does not cease to offer them.

In his book, *Callings: Finding and Following an Authentic Life*, Gregg Levoy tells the story of listening to music on the car radio as he drives home one night. The song playing is the *Queen of Hearts*, and as he exits his car in the driveway of his home, there before him lies the playing card, the queen of hearts. He ignores the strange occurrence, but the queen keeps turning up in front of him in improbable locations, such as a sand dune in Oregon and on a mountain in Colorado, six miles from the closest trailhead.

It finally dawns on him that the universe is giving him a message, one he ultimately unravels as his need to get out of his head and develop more feminine qualities: less preaching, more inner life within himself, more intuition, and less intellect. Once he interpreted the message, the queen of hearts vanished.

Chapter 15

Dreams

"A dream tells you where you are, not what to do; or, by placing you where you are, it tells you what you are doing."
          – James Hillerman, *The Dream and the Underworld*

Dreams often appear as the most familiar messengers to people. The ancients called them messages from the gods. I frequently dream of a house that represents my life. By examining this house in detail, I know what is going on underneath my public persona. Also, when I journey for a client, I often see them as a house. This makes sense when we consider that our body is the home of our spirit.

A few years ago, I dreamed my house burned down. That didn't mean I was dying. It did, however, bring a strong message that my life had major changes in store. In a period of eighteen months, I quit my job, bought a condo on the Columbia River, published my first book, and started writing this one. The dream was accurate.

Dreams can carry subtle or overt messages. I recall one where I was going the wrong way down a street in a too-small car that someone else was driving. That was very easy to decipher. I needed to take control of my own life, enlarge my sphere of activity, and go in a different direction. Around the same time, I had another dream about a teacher with whom I had begun to study. She appeared to be pregnant in the dream but then removed a false belly. In another dream, she wore a ring with beautiful stones, but the center stone on which the outer stones should be based was missing. Her many skills were not centered on love; she was obviously not a teacher I would want to follow.

Yet dreams are not always obvious. Sometimes, a dream is difficult to interpret, and we question how it applies to us. For example, one time, I dreamed of someone close to me. He appeared as himself in the dream, and so did the other players. He was running from one to the other, like a lapdog, while I was sitting alone in the corner of the room. While I saw that clearly, I could not recognize the obvious message. Later, it was an easy interpretation: He was catering to others' desires, not considering mine or ours as a couple.

Some dreams can appear even more obtuse. You might elect to draw as well as write down those dreams. You will need to look at each element and determine the meanings of the symbols and actions.

If you share your dreams with another seeking enlightenment, dream expert Robert Moss suggests that they preface their interpretations with the phrase "If it were my dream, I would …" You remain the ultimate source of knowing of your dream. It comes from a place deep within your psyche.

Many dreams have layers of meaning; you may understand the message on the top layer yet not comprehend the second until months or years later. Timing can also be an issue. I had a dream that was to come into fruition in four years. It took fourteen years, but it came in exactly as it had been shown me in the dream. Another dream didn't have an ending, and I was told it could work out either way; it took three years to culminate. Apparently, information may be exact but timing isn't.

Many excellent books exist regarding dreams. Try Robert A. Johnson's *Inner Work* and Robert Moss's *The Three "Only" Things: Tapping the Power of Dreams, Coincidence & Imagination*, or other works by either author.

Jill Mellick's *The Art of Dreaming: Tools for Creative Dream Work* offers techniques with movement, the use of artistic methods, word play, and writing. In her book is the following quote, which explains her reason for using art with dreams:

"Both dreams and the ritual arts manifest and mediate transpersonal energies. Both are forms of enactment expressing the depths of existence and energies flowing from the source through life. ... To use processes suggested by one to illuminate the other may permit us to relate to the dream in terms that do not lurch it from its matrix, yet facilitate and develop participant witnessing in the dreamer."

-Sylvia Brinton Perea's *Dream Design*, quoted in Nathan Schwartz-Salant and Murray Stein, eds., *Dreams in Analysis.*

Painting, sand painting, mask making, poetry, and other artistic tools help individuals to see deeper into their dreams and life as they are currently living it.

When an artist friend of mine was going through a divorce, she found herself taking a nap, getting up, and going downstairs to paint. A series of large watercolor paintings resulted. The first painting was stiff and ridged, hard lines of dark browns and muddy reds and oranges predominated. One had only to look at the painting to feel the pain it portrayed. But each watercolor softened in form and color; each painting seemed to flow a little more. I have the original of the final painting in my living room. It has wonderful shades of green, blue and white, the colors as fresh and flowing as springtime when winter's ice breaks. The series expressed her emotions as she progressed through the divorce, which I believe helped her deal with the experience itself.

Here is a poem I once wrote after a dream about where I currently was in my life. Writing this poem made it more real and understandable to me. Use whatever art form works for you. These two examples demonstrate only two possibilities of artistic expression.

I Dream a House

I dream of a house
with ugly high foundation.
No light shines from within.
Small and plain it stands alone,
a weedy garden by its door.

A huge tree grows before its window
no view is visible beyond.
The rooms are cramped;
The house is dark.
And I am so forlorn.

Months later I chop down that tree
and sunlight floods within.
I discover a river winding past
with houses on its shore.
And a winter garden by my door.

I also encourage you to keep a special dream journal, but avoid relying on a dream dictionary. Instead of turning to a dream dictionary, ask, "What does it mean to me, the dreamer?" A snake is a symbol of kundalini energy to some, but may mean the garden of evil and temptation to another, the shedding of the past, an aspect of humbleness to yet another since a snake crawls upon the earth, or even some other meaning.

In closing: For those of you who think you do not dream, this is not true. You simply are not recalling them. Keep a pen and journal or a voice recorder by your bed, and record your dream at once, or it will leave you. Go to bed with a promise to the universe to record your dreams. It may take a while to develop the ability to recall your dreams, but we all can. And once developed, dreams show us many important things.

Dreams can reveal the future, tell us where we are wrong, warn us of danger, and offer deeper insights than our rational brain can furnish.

Chapter 16

Books

I suspect all of us have had occasions where we just "happened" to pick up a book that had a message for us. I've had unopened books on my shelf for years only to pick one up and find exactly what I need inside it. Often, it contains something I can understand now but wouldn't have understood if I had read it when I bought it.

And there are some books that are like an onion. You read and understand things on one level, only to find when you go back and reread the book, another layer is added to your understanding. Books often have layers and layers of things to share with the reader.

You might try the technique of picking up a book and opening it anywhere. That method frequently delivers a message. Even better is a book that jumps off the shelf into your hands because it is so eager to deliver its message. In fact, written words anywhere can give you a message, if you are aware.

A journal is a specific type of book that can give you rich messages. A journal can be used with art techniques. Instead of saying you are tense or angry, draw the emotion. Seeing it gives an entirely different picture of your emotion, and often a way to untangle it.

Reframing an event in your journal, helps as well. I explain reframing in my book, The Magic Theater: Your Personal Journal, as looking at a situation or thought from different perspective. After all, it is not the event that creates our unhappiness, but how we think of the event and, thus, how we approach it. Use your journal to go deeper into your problems as well as your dreams. The Magic Theater has many exercises to help you be more aware of thoughts and behaviors and to make changes where you wish.

Chapter 17

People

Everyone is our mirror, so we are constantly being given messages. Other people reflect parts of our consciousness and give us a chance to see ourselves as we truly are. The qualities we admire and those we dislike are both reflected.

If we react negatively to something another says or does, it often signals something in our shadow has been triggered. We need to turn within and see why it disturbed us so much that we reacted. Ask, "What in me responds so strongly to this situation?" Dialogue with it in your journal. Some experts suggest you dialogue your logical questions and comments with your dominant hand and the responses you receive from the universe with your nondominant hand.

This concept of mirrors was not clear to me when I first started on the spiritual path. I would find myself reacting to someone or something and think, *How can this reflect me?* Only on close examination would I find that quality within myself. That quality perhaps was not as strong as (or perhaps stronger than) the person mirroring me—but it was there. And once I was aware, it could be changed or encouraged.

Since we often are our own worst critics, the ability to see myself possessing the qualities I'd admired in others proved as difficult as seeing myself with those qualities I felt were negative. However, as I grew calmer, produced less drama, and became more compassionate and less judgmental, others began to remark on the admirable qualities in me. My ninety-year-old mother once told me, "I like to be with you. Just sitting here with you makes me feel good." Her comment surprised me. I hadn't noticed the quality she saw in me.

It is easier to mirror back calmness or love when someone exudes those qualities to us. We seem to automatically mirror them. Other times, we admire something in another, perhaps their courage, when we don't see courage in ourselves. If this is the case, claim it and act courageously when courage is called for. Be assured that that seed of courage exists somewhere inside of you, or you wouldn't recognize it. Being aware of our human mirrors and the messages they can present is one of the quicker ways we can grow. Learning to recognize yourself in others is not that hard; those messages are a rich source of growth.

Also, do not fear what is often referred to as your shadow. Shadows contain both strength and weakness. In fact, what is in your shadow usually turns into some of your strongest positive gifts, once you are aware of it and work with your shadow. There are excellent books on shadow work by Robert Johnson, Connie Zweig, Debbie Ford, and Robert Bly.

Be aware also that messages can be delivered through strangers. A friend's nephew had decided to go ahead with surgery on his foot, much to my friend's dismay. All the logical reasons to forgo the operation were rejected by the young man until he heard a woman in the checkout line ahead of him at the grocery store tell the clerk of the same operation and the problems she had from it. This, a message from a stranger, is synchronicity at its best!

Chapter 18

Animals

Animals often deliver messages. In the shamanic tradition, when we see an animal three or four times, it is offering to become a totem for us. Totems act as guides and protectors, and they also offer us qualities that we need to uncover in our self. Their coming gives us access to those qualities that we may not be aware of needing and may need to develop. For instance, I received a mountain goat on one occasion. It appeared that I needed to be sure-footed in the next step of my journey.

Shamans traditionally meet their totems in the journey process, but I am convinced these helpers also appear to us in everyday life. They can come to you with messages, just as the crows came to me.

I can be as obtuse as anyone at times. The first three times the crows came, I was aware it was unusual but didn't think much more about it. My first visit occurred while I was working at my desk in Colorado. I have a sliding glass door to the deck in front of my desk, and a crow appeared on the deck railing ten feet from me.

"Wow!" I thought as I quietly got up to grab my camera and take a picture. But the crow took off as I approached the door.

A few days later, three crows appeared in the trees at the edge of my yard. I was aware of them but gave them no thought, other than to snap a photo of one in the tree. A week or ten days later, when working in the dining room-kitchen area of my home, a murder of crows appeared in a tree about twenty feet from where I stood. This time, I found myself impressed by the crows' sheer numbers and their intention that I see them, but I did nothing about it.

Summer came, and the seasons passed into fall, winter, and spring, yet no more crows appeared. I left in May and took up residence in Astoria, with no crows in sight. Well, no live crows. I must admit that when I went to the Saturday Market in Ilwaco, Washington, across the river from Astoria, I found myself drawn to a booth with handsome life-sized, metal-sculpted crows. I bought one for the deck of my Colorado home.

However, about a month after the purchase of my black metal crow, live crows appeared again. This time, two crows joined me on my walk into Astoria's Maritime Museum. They swooped down about three feet from me. One crow walked up parallel to me and kept me company for a few steps, each of us occasionally glancing at the other. Then it flew away, and the second crow fluttered across the trolley lines to me and walked briefly at my side. I continued into the museum, but at this point, my attention had been captured by the thoughts of how beautiful the birds were and how unusual it was to have them visit me.

Two days later, as I worked at my desk again, while glancing out at the Columbia River in front of me from time to time, I saw a crow flit by. A few minutes later, the crow came by a bit more slowly and, closer to my window. This time as it passed, the bird emitted a loud "Cawwww." I walked out onto the small balcony of my condo, and the crow, perched on a piling below me, looked up in my direction.

"Okay," I said. "I got it. I need to research crow qualities." That day and the next, while I read everything I could put my hands on about crows, I saw crows everywhere: playing on the lawn at the corner of the condo, flying high over the parking lot. People told me there were lots of crows in the area, but these were the first I'd seen.

Then, almost overnight, the crows vanished, their message that I had to speak my truth had been delivered. Other than the black metal crow on my deck railing, it was a long time before I saw a crow again.

As you progress in understanding animals' work in your energetic field, you may begin to see their energy at work in others. I recall looking at a woman in a workshop once and seeing a turtle within her; her need for protection and shyness were evident.

Animals in our daily encounters sense energy more easily than humans usually do. If animals start to act differently around you,

you will know your energy has changed. The vibes you give off are different.

When I went for a wolf tour in Colorado, a group of us took the special step of entering the space the alpha wolf shared with his mate. We were told he might select one of us as special, someone he would like for his clan. If this happened, he would lick us on the lips. The woman next to me was so excited about this and wanted to be chosen, but I though little about it and felt less than eager to have a wolf lick me on the lips.

When we entered the compound, the wolf walked over to us and started to walk beside me; as we went further into the enclosure, we sat on large boulders, and the wolf kissed me on the lips. While I was with him, he was very protective of me, not even allowing his mate to get too close. Was I thrilled? You bet. He noticed something in me that I had not known was there.

Chapter 19

Our Physical Body

We all have felt bodily symptoms, and we often ignore them. We can recognize the simple ones. We are tired; it is time to go to sleep. We are hungry; it is time to eat. Bodily pain means something is wrong and needs our attention. But the body gives us more feedback than this. And we need to be more aware and grateful, for this aspect is very individualized to each of us.

Everything is created from energy. We are energy, but we sometimes forget that fact and fail to consider that not all energies match. Have you ever walked into a place or been around someone who made you feel uncomfortable? Can you recall feelings of impending danger or revulsion? The cells of our bodies have minds and memories, and physical symptoms are attempting to tell us something. Pay attention the next time your body is trying to speak to you.

A close friend of mine let the woman he deeply loved go. Shortly afterward, he was rushed to the hospital with what was thought to be a heart attack. It turned out after medical tests had been completed that he hadn't had a heart attack. His body, however, had reacted to his emotionally broken heart.

Another friend who looked back over the years of her marriage realized she was getting sick because when she was ill, her husband paid more attention to her.

I started having knee problems because I didn't want to move forward on the path that I knew the universe wanted me to take. It took me two knee replacements and ten years to get serious about what I needed to do. And by the way, I found I loved the path once I entered it with commitment. Can you imagine the price I paid for not listening to that message sooner? At this point, if I were Aesop, I would say "and the moral of the story is, learn to identify what your body's message is and trust it."

For more detail on your body's messages, look at most, if not all, of the books by Louise Hay of Hay House. You may also like to consider Caroline Myss' *Anatomy of the Spirit* and *Why People Don't Heal and How They Can.*

Chapter 20

Messages Come in Many Ways

Be aware. Messages come in myriad ways. You might look for events that are repetitious. A friend remarked on her Facebook page that her glasses broke again, and every time that happened, it meant she wasn't looking at something clearly. Look at synchronicities, repeating numbers, and unexpected occurrences for the messages they may carry. Boredom is a message. And being in the flow is its opposite message.

Joseph Campbell told us to follow our bliss. That is a good way to measure a message from any person or institution; it needs to feel right for you. Our families, schools, and culture give us lots of messages. Every religion gives messages, but not all the messages agree. How will you know which is right? You will feel its rightness in your body. Peace and comfort will arrive with it. It will fit you. And it may be persistent, like my crows and Levoy's queen of hearts.

I've had a message delivered by a voice from within, another given me by the wolf, and some revealed in something someone said to me or something I read or saw in a movie. I have been carried away by classical music to receive messages from the universe. My dreams and shamanic journeys have been the clearest and most frequent ways for me to receive messages. However, a list of how messages can be given is endless. The spirit of the world is a mystery, but it is real, and it does love us, each and every one of us.

Prologue
My Thanks

This small book would not be complete without mentioning the crew of talented people involved. In the beginning, Will and Barbie Cassity, Mary Hope, Paul Bakke, and Dave and Peggy Stevens encouraged me to write my story of living on the Columbia River and offered valuable comments and assistance in this endeavor.

A special thank you to Gregg Levoy for his wonderful book *Callings* and his experience with the queen of hearts, which he so graciously gave me permission to use.

I would be remiss not to mention Leanne Kemper and Lloyd Keniston, who both spent many hours attempting to get that perfect photo into the perfect size. In the end, however, I elected to turn the photos into chalk illustrations. Eva at the Book of Khaleesi graciously made that transformation.

Many of the photographs that are the basis for the illustrations were taken by me. My daughter Kara Bakke took the rest of the photographs involved in the book with one exception, the gorgeous photograph of the heron, which separates the two sections of the book, is the work of Kevin Danishefsky.

I needed a new author's photo and met a new friend in the shape of the photographer, Teresa of Teresa Lee Photography in Colorado Springs.

A very talented web designer and the webmaster of wwwdrjillbakke. com, Therese Wells, took on the task of creating the book's cover and redesigning my website to reflect my truth.

Nikki Busch, who did the original edit, and the person who did the final edit for Lulu deserve mention. Lulu doesn't give their editor's name to the author; so, even though the individual appears as a Jane or John Doe in this prologue, I want to acknowledge the valuable line editing and formatting that was provided.

Finally, none of this would be complete without one last mention, my contacts at Lulu. Thank you for patiently standing by me while I sorted out the problems with photos, illustrations, formatting and all the little details that go into making a book. Your patience sustained me.

If it takes a village to raise a child, it takes a parcel of helpers to produce a book. I could not have published this book without the assistance of each of you. Your input, encouragement, and skillful help are gratefully appreciated. Thank you, my friends.

Jill

About the Author

Jill Hance Bakke, Ed.D. says Astoria, with its nearness to the Pacific Ocean and living on the incredible Columbia River, is like coming home again after a long drought. A nature lover, with training in shamanism, hypnosis, and traditional psychology, she is the author of *The Magic Theater: Your Personal Journal*, which is geared to self-knowledge and change. She currently splits her time between the Oregon coast and Colorado. You can learn more about her at www.drjillbakke.com.